HAROLD KLEMP

TOUCHING THE FACE OF GOD

HAROLD KLEMP

ECKANKAR
Minneapolis

ABOUT THIS BOOK: *Touching the Face of God* is compiled from Harold Klemp's writings. These selections originally appeared in his books published by Eckankar.

Touching the Face of God
Copyright © 2006 ECKANKAR

Printed in USA
Compiled by John Kulick
Edited by Patrick Carroll, Joan Klemp, and Anthony Moore
Cover photo: Calla Lilies #27, 2004.
Photograph copyright © 2004 Huntington Witherhill
Text photo by Robert Huntley
Cover design by Doug Munson

Library of Congress Cataloging-in-Publication Data
Klemp, Harold.
    Touching the face of God / Harold Klemp.
        p. cm.
    ISBN 1-57043-231-7 (hardcover : alk. paper)
    I. Eckankar (Organization) I. Title.
    BP605.E3K57475 2006
    299'.93—dc22
                                            2006002662

♾ This paper meets the requirements of ANSI/NISO Z39.48-1992 (Permanence of Paper).

CONTENTS

DEAR READER

Prepare for an opportunity to transform the way you experience God in your life. That is the purpose of this remarkable book, the fourth volume in Harold Klemp's award-winning Immortality of Soul series.

In *Touching the Face of God*, Harold Klemp encourages each of us to recognize that we are Soul, an infinitely creative divine being.

Discover how daily practice of contemplative techniques, the Spiritual Exercises of ECK, helps you receive guidance via direct communication with Divine Spirit.

Take one quote each day, and contemplate its meaning. Ask Divine Spirit to show you how to recognize Its guidance in your life. The keys to touching the face of God and getting the most from life are at your fingertips.

GETTING THE MOST FROM LIFE

*P*eople who have the best relationship with life and understand the spiritual realities and God more clearly than the average person—no matter their financial situation, rich or poor—are generally able to be happy with themselves and others.

$\mathcal{Y}$our daily life is the spiritual life. So often someone will say, "If you will take away this pain and give me a spiritual healing or give me money, I'll be better able to live the spiritual life." They don't realize these are the experiences that will give them spiritual understanding. We learn compassion. This is part of our experience here.

$\mathcal{Y}$ou find when you overstep a law of life, life has a way of putting the law into action and bringing it back to you. We know this as the Law of Cause and Effect. Saint Paul referred to it in the Christian Bible when he said, "Whatsoever a man soweth, that shall he also reap."

*W*e each choose our own state of consciousness. It takes a while for many individuals to recognize this. We make our own worlds. What we are today is the sum total of everything we have thought or been throughout the ages.

*W*e surrender our fears, our cares, and our worries. In the meantime, we plan our daily life.

We visualize something on the inner, and then we set out to do whatever we can to bring that plan into being. There are many people who have thousands of ideas, but the truly rare person is the one who can figure out what he has to do in the physical world to make his dream come true.

When the Spirit of God comes into your life, It will uplift you and give understanding into the problems and joys of your daily life. It gives direction, and for many this is the first time they have found it.

It gives meaning and reason to life and answers to questions such as why a baby dies when it's only five days old or why an individual is required to suffer for years and years before he finally dies. It gives answers, because understanding reincarnation and the Law of Karma gives us a view that goes beyond the borders where scientists dare not tread.

We work as individuals in a spiritual sense, learning the laws of Spirit to make our life a little bit easier, to gain understanding, and to take away the fear of death.

One of the purposes of Eckankar, Religion of the Light and Sound of God, is to give us a spiritual understanding of who and what we are.

When today is different from yesterday, we accept it. This is called living in the detached state of consciousness. We accept what we have here in the moment, without any regrets for the past.

*B*uild your spiritual foundation carefully so when the psychic waves come, bringing doubt and fear, problems, and health situations, you will be strong enough to see and know why you are going through this, and that it will pass. Whatever is here today must one day pass. It's the nature of life. Spring gives us the example: Nature renews itself each year; it renews all life.

*W*e take our steps on the spiritual path; we climb the ladder to God.

The grace of God does not descend upon us. This is something religions often do not understand. They feel the grace of God comes to us merely because we ask. It does in a way, but first we must earn it. We must make at least some effort before the grace of God comes to us; but when it does, we are lifted up into it.

A person who lives in the holiness of the moment is always looking for the potential of whatever that moment may bring. Always.

As Soul, you owe yourself the experience of going out in life and getting the richest, fullest experiences you can.

RECOGNIZING OURSELVES AS SOUL

*S*ome of the religious teachings believe body and Soul are one and the same. In Eckankar we believe Soul comes in and takes on the physical body as a temple to use so It can move in this physical world.

God created Soul outside the parameters of time and space. Soul is without beginning or ending.

Some people believe Soul comes into existence at the birth of the infant, but this is not quite an accurate belief. If it were, then Soul would not be eternal, because Soul would have a beginning in this finite world. But Soul has existed before the birth of the child.

What is the relationship of Soul to God? Soul is the essence of God. Soul is not God—It could never be God. We can never be one with God, although we can be one with Spirit.

As Soul we are looking only for experience, whether it's in this world or in the other worlds.

*W*e are here to learn how to let Soul get in control of our lower selves. We're up and down. Some days we're doing great, other days we're not. But the worst thing we can do is feel guilty and start criticizing or blaming ourselves, saying, I have sinned.

An interesting definition of sin comes from the Greeks: *hamartanein*. It means to err, to miss the mark. Rather than implying an afterlife spent in hell, it simply means to miss the mark.

We recognize that there are some people who have unfolded more; but Soul, in quality, is Soul. The difference in consciousness is the difference in unfoldment. It doesn't make one person bigger or another person smaller—as Soul.

*W*e're all scrambling. It's called spiritual survival. And we learn that to survive, we do whatever is necessary to make something work, especially when we see it is part and parcel of our spiritual self, the Soul body.

*S*oul is an individual and unique en-tity. Each of you has had different experi-ences up until now, so each of you is going to have different experiences in the future. This is how it must be.

*S*oul is multidimensional. It shares all the aspects of God. Soul can be everywhere at all times, and all places at the same time. This is that part of God that you are.

Begin remembering your dreams to get an idea of who and what you are as Soul.

*T*he tears and the sorrows life gives us are for our own spiritual development and unfoldment. By development and unfoldment, I mean the growing recognition of ourselves in the true state—as Soul, the divine spark of God.

*S*oul's mission is to become a Co-worker with God. It is simply that and nothing more.

How truth is taught

How is truth taught? Spirit works through us, but It also teaches through nature and through the lessons of history.

*O*ur search for happiness is actually the search for God; it is a search for the Golden Age when Soul dwelt in the high worlds of Spirit and the high worlds of God.

*T*he very slender hold we have on historical truth is based on man's ability to write. In the absence of writing materials or skills, he has to pass down fables and stories to his sons about the greatness of past cultures.

*H*istory proves there is no permanency in the civilizations of man, nor in the religions of man. The only permanence is in the inner direction that comes from the heart center.

*A*s we start out in our own searchings, we may pray to God for this or that. As we go farther, we learn much prayer is asking God to change what God has already allowed. Maybe God allowed this for our own learning.

And then our prayers change from "God, take away this illness" to "God, let me understand why this has been given to me." In other words, we begin asking for spiritual understanding.

$\mathcal{W}$e are looking for a higher permanence than the physical body and human history. Soul yearns to leave the limits of time and space that encompass the events of the earth. To leave behind the karma which binds us here, to gain liberation of Soul, to gain the attributes of God: wisdom, power, and freedom.

We are trying to learn the laws of Spirit, and until we do, we make karma. And as long as we make karma, we have troubles—because we're learning.

No person on this earth has all the answers, including myself, because as soon as he does, it's time to go.

*S*pirit will work with each person, with each one of you, in a way that is right for you.

*J*esus said there were some among his disciples who would not die until they saw the kingdom of heaven. And then he said, "The kingdom of God cometh not with observation: Neither shall they say, Lo here! or, lo there! for, behold, the kingdom of God is within you."

So two points were made: the kingdom of heaven is within you, not somewhere out there; and there were some standing there who would see the kingdom of heaven before they died.

To see the Light and hear the Sound of God is to experience spiritual upliftment that pulls you into the worlds of knowing. Here you become aware, consciously, of the divine laws of Spirit and can use this knowledge to wend your way through life.

I encourage those of you who are not having experiences in the dream state to keep your eyes open. Look around you, because once you are linked up with Divine Spirit, Spirit begins to work—to uplift, to strengthen, and to straighten out your life.

We learn very soon that no matter what happens to us, the purpose is to teach us more about the laws of Spirit.

THE VOICE OF GOD

What are the Light and Sound of God? They are the two aspects that Christianity has called the Holy Spirit. This is the Voice of God.

The Voice of God comes down through creation as Light and Sound. We take these two aspects of life for granted.

*I*t would be great if each of you would have direct experience with the Light and Sound of God, where you would actually see this Light. Sometimes It comes as a blue light, other times you can see It as orange, white, or yellow. It depends upon the level, or the heaven, or the state of consciousness you are working from at that moment.

This Light of God is the upliftment which comes to purify Soul so Soul can fly free.

*T*here are many sounds of Spirit, which usually are heard as music or something similar to a sound of nature. One of them is the buzzing of bees. Another sound is a humming, which can be heard at a different level. Or you can hear the flute of God.

The importance of these sounds in our spiritual unfoldment is that when we hear the Sound of God, Spirit is uplifting and purifying us in our state of consciousness.

The Light and Sound opens the doorway of love. Love is the doorway to spiritual freedom. Before you can realize the gift of spiritual freedom, you must go through that doorway and have the love of God transform your life.

We look for experiences and direct knowledge with the Light and Sound of God because this is communication with the deity: God speaks through the Light and Sound.

*W*hen you are looking to find God, first you think, What is my ideal? Then you plan what you can do to get there. Whatever path or personal discipline you choose is right for you.

More importantly, you go deep within yourself through the contemplative techniques, and you come in contact with the Light and Sound of God. And when you come in contact with this Voice, It will lead you to your home. This is the Ocean of Love and Mercy, which we know as God.

The Spiritual Exercises of ECK help us come in contact with the Light and Sound of God. These contemplative techniques give us confidence in ourselves. We learn that we are Soul, we are eternal. Then we know with certainty that we live forever, that death cannot destroy us.

*T*here's a great distinction between meditation and contemplation. Meditation teaches you to go inwardly and sit quietly. In so doing, you become passive and quiet.

Contemplation is an active way. We sit down for twenty minutes, sing a sacred name of God such as HU (pronounced like the word *hue*), and look for the Light and Sound of God. As It comes through, it is not meant to be just one experience for our whole lifetime; It comes in many different ways, at many different times.

*T*he power of HU can benefit everyone, whether they are Muslim or Christian or of any other belief. It doesn't change one's religion, but it will enhance it.

*A*s we begin to get this Light and Sound in our life, it shows in how we conduct our daily affairs. Our daily life is a reflection of what happens inwardly.

If we set a goal for a project, we ought to get a grasp of spiritual principles from the experience. These experiences help us succeed in the sense that they take us to the next step in life.

*S*ome of you are fortunate to have conscious experience with the Light and Sound of God. This simply means that you are awakening in the other worlds. What you bring back to earth is more love and a greater understanding of yourself than you had before.

THE PATH OF PERSONAL EXPERIENCE

What prepares you for the true path of God? The experiences of life.

*H*ere is a question for you: Is it possible to get so many experiences in life that you become jaded, dull, and bored?

It should never happen. It would mean that you are refusing the avenues of growth to which Spirit is leading you.

*U*ntil you have your dreams aligned with your actions, you are not fulfilling your destiny. If you can dream something, you can do it. Talking isn't going to get you there.

*T*here is a saying that if you live the spiritual life, you'll never suffer boredom.

When we are bored, it's simply because we are refusing to grow.

*T*he human consciousness has a natural inclination toward lethargy and procrastination. This is because of attachment, which is one of the mind passions. We learn to work with it. In your personal life you learn to set goals.

Set little goals, any goals, just so that you do something. Soul is here to gain experience, and you're not going to get a lot of experience without doing something.

*P*eople join the religion most suitable to them, because it is right that they belong there. For this reason, we must have a certain amount of tolerance for each other. This is why we don't have the right to put down a religious path simply because it differs from our own.

To do so is to mock the plan of God, which allows for so many different ways of expression.

*T*he Holy Spirit isn't going to feed experiences to you on a silver spoon just to delight your senses. It won't send you one phenomenal experience after another to keep your interest. Life isn't like that.

It doesn't put us in the receiver position, constantly waiting for life to do something for us. Somewhere we have to take the step.

A true spiritual healing first heals the spiritual condition that caused the symptom to appear in the physical body. But this does not belie the fact that sometimes the body simply wears out.

When we have fulfilled our mission here, it's time to go on to another classroom, to another mansion in the other worlds.

*F*ar too often we ask God, Please take away my sorrow and trouble, and we overlook the reason for the problem.

The purpose of difficulties is to make us strong, to give us experience. Experience for what? The mission of Soul. The mission of every Soul, whether It understands this or not, is to become a Co-worker with God.

*L*ove gives a shortcut to heaven. If you do one little thing each day for love and love alone, without any expectation of reward, you're going to find that life gives you more and more.

*E*ckankar is not the intellectual path where we sit around and make more and more plans. It is the path of doing—the path of personal experience. It's a marriage of plans with action.

THE GREATER TRUTH

Whatever path to God you follow ought to make you able to stand on your own feet here as well as in the inner worlds; here and now, in this lifetime, before you drop the body in death.

If the path isn't able to do that, then you ought to keep looking until you find one that gives you this ability.

What we are trying to do on the path of Eckankar is to find out what this life we are living actually means and how the spiritual consciousness can make it better—both now and after we step through the veil into the true worlds of the greater Light and the greater Sound of Spirit.

In this world, it sometimes takes strength. It's easy enough to speak about peace when you're basking under the umbrella of strength, but without that umbrella, you would be like a six-year-old in the school-yard.

In the spiritual worlds it's very much the same way. No matter how sweet and tender we try to be, if we are ignorant of the spiritual laws of God, we are at the mercy of life.

*M*y job is to point out there is a way for you to contact the divine essence of God. You can contact the Holy Spirit and guide yourself directly. You don't have to rely on the words and teachings of a person just because he speaks with authority.

*M*an is looking for two things: peace and love. He wants happiness, and he looks for it everywhere. This desire stems from his dim memory of the Golden Age of man, long since past.

The secret teachings are the teachings of the Holy Spirit. It is sometimes difficult to tie in the divine teachings with the everyday things that go on here on earth.

Reincarnation clears up a lot of mysteries. This is why Eckankar has something to offer you.

*N*o matter how difficult life in this world gets, we know we are Soul and this is just one of the many bodies we have worn throughout all time. If we haven't finished our lessons, when the dust settles we can come back for another round.

But if we learn the way to be raised in consciousness, we can get off this wheel of reincarnation.

When you step onto the path and ask Spirit to come into your life and give you greater unfoldment, It will. The Sound and Light pour into you whether or not you're conscious of it. It will pour in for perhaps a year or two, sometimes longer; then when you get filled up, you have to learn what to do with It.

This is the next step, this learning how to give in some way that suits you. It won't be the same for any two people, nor will the way that you've chosen to serve hold forever. Then you have to find a new way.

*E*ckankar is a teaching that works directly with the Light and Sound. You can test it and find out for yourself. There are spiritual exercises mentioned in some of my books you can try. *The Spiritual Exercises of ECK* has one called "Listening for God."

If you are of the Christian faith and you're more comfortable with prayer, you can pray to God: "Show me Thy ways, show me Thy truth." When you have asked with a sincere heart, this will be brought to you.

Ask to be shown in a way that is right for you.

As the Living ECK Master, the spiritual leader of Eckankar, I have still another duty—to prod people into gaining an understanding, beyond blind faith, of the religion they are following. I'd rather see you reading the Bible than sitting on it. You will probably learn something in your studies. So many people who claim to follow the Bible have never really read it.

I'm not that interested in whether you follow the path of Eckankar, but I am interested in Soul becoming aware of Its true state, of Its divinity.

No matter what path you are on or what faith you follow, be the best there is in it, be the cream of the crop. Because until you are that, you haven't learned the lessons that you need to learn; and until they are learned, you will not be able to graduate to the next step and learn the greater truth.

FACING LIFE'S CHALLENGES

*A*s we go higher and raise ourselves in the spiritual consciousness, we are able to solve the problems of life. We are happy. We are at home in every environment.

*W*e have to face this life. The fact is, we do have problems. And our problems sometimes seem so heavy we cry for help to God, to the angels, or to anyone else who gives us at least a hope of lifting the burden, so we can face life with some measure of happiness, contentment, and peace.

This is what many of us are looking for in life.

*T*here are times we are given an abundance of Light and Sound, and there are times the Lord will withdraw these.

Why? For the strengthening of Soul. Saint John of the Cross called this the dark night of the Soul.

As we unfold, our potential for solving problems increases. This is simply because we have a closer, more intimate contact with the Light and the Sound of God. We expand in our circle of awareness.

*T*he creative process is actually a misnomer, because creation is finished and all we do is manifest what is already there. So you're not really creating a solution to the problem; you are manifesting something that is already there.

The potential of the rose is in the bud, but before you can see its beauty, the bud has to unfold.

*W*hen the creative imagination is working in you, life is right; you wake up in the morning to rainbows and sunshine. This means you are operating under the hand of God, as if you are living in the kingdom of heaven here and now.

*S*oul hasn't any problems; we have problems in our mental, emotional, or physical bodies. Soul hasn't any real problems to speak of.

It isn't concerned about a whole lot of things; It isn't concerned about how long we live, because Soul is eternal.

*S*alvation isn't for the physical body, it's for Soul. Here and now, while in the physical body, we are already learning how to move into the heavens in full consciousness and come back alive.

*W*hy is this ability to travel to the inner planes or heavens important? Very simply, it's because this knowledge helps you overcome the fear of death.

*W*hen you have gained power over the fear of death, there is nothing that can hold you back in this life. Problems become stepping-stones, not obstacles that trip you.

You become like the revered masters of the sacred writings. They too once walked this earth like you and me, but they learned the laws of Spirit and how to apply them to solve their own problems.

How to become a Master actually means something very similar to what merchants mean when they speak of added value. Another way to say it is that we take one step more than we have to, one step more than the average man.

THE SECRET TEACHINGS

*T*he secret teachings are not secret because they are hidden away somewhere or because I'm keeping them from you. They are secret because until one is ready for these teachings, he couldn't see them even if he tripped over them.

*I*t's best that truth come in a way you can handle. It might be through a book, or maybe a friend will come up to you and say, "I heard about this particular teaching."

It may be Eckankar, or it may be another teaching. It makes no difference.

All that a true spiritual teaching can give you is assurance of the eternal nature of Soul: that you live beyond the death of the physical body; that you are Soul, and you live forever. A sword can pierce the body but never Soul.

And if you know what you're doing, when you leave this body it's not much of a change.

*T*o be on the spiritual path means to follow this Wind of Change, which is Spirit.

If you are on a true path to God and you're unfolding in spiritual consciousness, changes are going to come into your life. They can't help but come. Things are going to be different. You may not know what's happening at first, but your friends will see a change in you.

*I*n living life, we often get to think-
ing we're so smart. But it seems that the more
intellectual one becomes, the harder it is for
him to see the spiritual essence of God—
the Light and Sound.

*W*hat does self-surrender in ECK mean? It means giving up all your cares, worries, and troubles to the Inner Master, to Spirit.

In a way, the leaders of each major religious teaching do the same thing for their followers, passing their cares and troubles on to Spirit. But it should only be done until one can learn how to do it for himself.

*T*here is a lot said about spiritual truths and about healing and everything else. Much of what you hear is foolishness, much of it is plain common sense.

It is up to us, through the knowledge of the spiritual laws, to figure out which is which.

*G*od created the lower worlds as a place for us to learn. We go ahead and do whatever we want to—and we pay the price. This is the divine Law of Cause and Effect.

*A*ll that the spiritual teachings can ever do for anybody is to show them how to make contact with the essence of God. Some call It the Holy Spirit, the Holy Ghost, or the Comforter. But whatever words you use, it means this unformed essence of God which comes as Light and Sound. You, as man, become the converter of It so that you can use It in your daily life.

You can use the Light to show you where the pitfalls are, and the Sound as a directional signal to show you the way back home to God.

*T*here really isn't a quick and easy road to heaven. In the teachings of Eckankar, we talk about the three steps to find the kingdom of heaven here and now. The first step is to find the Spiritual Traveler, who has experience in the other worlds and can help you out when you get in trouble.

Secondly, you need to find the Word of God, the Sound. This is the Music of God or the music of the spheres.

Then comes spiritual liberation.

The simple teaching of Eckankar is this: how to contact the Light and Sound of God, which have the power to give spiritual liberation in this lifetime.

THE LAW OF ECONOMY

The Law of Economy presupposes that everything we do is in harmony with the ECK (Holy Spirit), in harmony with life.

*T*he spiritual principle is that you get the most effect out of everything you do, and everything is turned to a spiritual effect. Through doing the spiritual exercises, the forces are no longer being scattered all over and wasted; they are now aligned in one direction, and that direction is home to God. So you see that the Law of Economy is important.

What usually isn't noticed is that the Law of Economy is expressed in everything we do and in the people we meet every day.

*T*he life of a country spans many decades, and karma doesn't necessarily come back tomorrow morning; it sometimes takes several years. In the meantime, everybody thinks they are getting a free ride. But they are forgetting the basic Law of Economy, which is the Law of Cause and Effect.

You pay for everything you get, both spiritually and materially.

We have to take full responsibility for our own lives. Once we do, we find that the problems we have are ones we can handle. Not only that, but we can often choose our problems. You may think if there were a choice between problems and no problems, you'd choose to have no problems, and I'd say you would be very wise. But this world doesn't run like that. It works by degrees, not absolutes.

It works like this: You are going to have problems, but you now have a choice as to how to handle them.

You may ask: If God is more powerful than Satan, why doesn't God stop this foolishness?

Because the negative power is an agent for God. His job is to act as the schoolmaster, following God's will. God said, "I've got a schoolroom of children here. Make sure these Souls get enough of an education so that when they graduate, they can go into the spiritual worlds and stand on their own two feet. Their destiny is to become Co-workers with God, helping me in the administration of my worlds."

An aspect of the Law of Economy is recognizing the weaknesses in any system on earth. This includes recognizing the weaknesses in our own character and makeup and working with them, as well as recognizing the same traits in other people and trying to work with them.

Earth will never be a heaven. Nor should you serve God for some cause other than your spiritual growth.

The Law of Economy makes an accommodation for every area of one's development: physical, psychic, mental, and spiritual.

*I*f something comes in a more attractive container, we're willing to pay more for it than its real value. Why? Because we like to think we're getting more.

In so doing, however, we are not using our resources to the fullest, which is part of the Law of Economy.

*T*he Law of Economy is an aspect of the ECK (Holy Spirit). It is always right, clean, and just. There is no pettiness in it, or spite or hatred.

*S*ervice means that every move, every thought, everything we do gets the best advantage. No matter what thought we have or what action we take, it results in the most productive deed we can do as Soul learning to become a Co-worker with God.

I have often referred to this service as the Law of Economy. It means that in every way we look for the best. We look to excel in every way.

*T*here is no shortcut unless one considers the Law of Economy, which is to take no more effort than is absolutely required to reach God.

MAINTAINING HARMONY AND BALANCE

*I*n the spiritual worlds, the law is: Fair is fair; I must give you freedom so you will give me freedom. And yet we know we must stand up to protect what we call the psychic space around us, so we don't allow other people to push their teachings on us.

No matter how far we go, we must always be careful about our spiritual values and balance.

*S*pirit often helps you at times when you may not even suspect you need help. But Spirit doesn't work like this all the time—only when you have put forth your best effort, and when you stay open to It.

You don't constantly say, Spirit, please help, because then you are placing the force, Spirit, outside of yourself. You are putting too much attention on this force as something that will take care of your personal responsibilities for you. So what happens? You end up shirking your own responsibility—your own Godhood.

111

$\mathcal{B}$e prepared so you are always at peace inside yourself, so you feel you are prepared; and know that the answer, or the solution, for every moment in your life is at hand in one way or another.

As long as you are patient and look to the Sound and Light, which may come as a gentle nudge, which may come as a feeling, you will be prepared.

If we can learn to put aside the fear of death, we find a joyousness in this life which then helps us make a very natural step into our next life.

*T*he purpose of the negative power is to work as a part of the divine plan. The devil is of a negative nature but still working the purpose of God.

When we have troubles, we like to put the blame on the devil or somebody else because it's an easy way out. Then we don't have to say, My words and actions have caused my own troubles.

*T*here really is no hurry. When you first begin on a spiritual path of any kind, you are so enthusiastic that you want to go as fast as you can. You're actually opening yourself to Spirit.

If you open up too fast, you can cause many problems in your life: money problems, health problems, everything. This is why I generally encourage people to go slowly.

Dreams are a starting point for many who wish to begin the spiritual journey to God and do it in the easiest possible way. Dreams taught me to face myself, let me see the future, and took me to the heavens of God.

If we can remember that Soul is an atom of God, that our relationship with the Divine Being is always one-on-one, then we have made a substantial step.

No longer is it important what people think about what we do. Every act has a consequence, and we recognize the consequences of our actions. But instead of weighing each action, we now work with the simplicity of Spirit. We listen to the heart, and then we say, Yes, I can do this, or No, I will not do that. Our life becomes simpler and more straightforward.

*I*f you want to lift yourself to a higher state of consciousness—so the political issues, the family issues, the social issues of the day do not throw you out of balance, so that you can find a happier, more contented life while you're living here—sing HU, the most beautiful prayer.

HU can protect. HU can give love. HU can heal. It can give peace of mind. That doesn't mean forever. It just means that if you face a crisis of some kind or another, remember to sing HU. Sing HU to yourself, or sing it out loud if no one's around.

*W*hat we are aiming for is not to avoid the roller-coaster effect of life, but to gain the middle path. This means the path of moderation, the balanced outlook, the spiritual viewpoint that no matter what happens, the sorrows of life will not bury us forever. When loved ones leave in death, we cry—but not forever. We are able to face life knowing that they will still live on in full consciousness.

We know that the divine cause, the Divine Being, has put us here to learn something. It is up to us to go out into life and find out what it is.

*E*ach Soul is an individual and unique being. We have two parts to our lower nature: the positive and the negative. When we get to the Soul Plane, we find that these two parts become one. This is called the self-recognition state, what the Greeks referred to when they said, Know thyself. Up until this time, knowing the self has meant merely knowing the ego, or the little self, rather than our true spiritual nature.

Our consciousness changes when we reach the Soul Plane; we now have an outlook on life that is balanced.

THE SELF-RECOGNITION OF TRUTH

We are told on the spiritual path to seek first the Kingdom of God. This is the mission of Soul: to become a Co-worker with God.

What we want to do is contact the Voice of God, which is the Holy Spirit, the ECK. This Voice of God can be known through the Light and Sound that uplifts us so we can reach into the high states of spiritual consciousness. No longer bound by the hand of destiny, we then become spiritually free to mark our own course for this lifetime and into the worlds beyond.

*T*his Sound that comes from the ECK has a purifying element which removes the impurities of Soul. It brings an understanding of how our actions have caused our problems. It also gives an indication of what we can do to unfold, and how to figure out the way to do things right.

When a problem comes up, we don't just say, Oh, no! We look to see the reason or the lesson behind it. What can I learn from it? How has it made me stronger? We are interested in becoming the mature Soul that can go on to become a Co-worker with God.

*S*oul is creative, infinitely creative. Our creative imagination is our gift from God. The imagination is the God-spark, the part of us that makes us like God. And you can direct it toward whatever needs improvement in your life.

When you have a great creative ability, consciously or unconsciously, you have been lifted in your state of consciousness. In the dream state or in another manner, you have been taken into one of the heavens.

*Y*ou find that the other worlds are natural and full of joy; and when you have the knowledge that there is no death, you no longer have the fear of death. When you realize you can come back to the body without this fear holding you back, you find your creative imagination begins to blossom. There are no more blocks in your personal life as you set your goals for material success and spiritual unfoldment.

*S*pirit wants to uplift us so that we develop what we call the spiritual consciousness, or Self-Realization. This is the self-recognition of truth: to know who and what we are and what our mission in this life may be.

When we have achieved this state of consciousness, then our next goal is God-Realization and reaching the kingdom of heaven in this lifetime.

*T*ake your share of drubbings, because within each lesson is hidden the seed of truth which is needed for you to take the step that follows.

When you can live your life fully, under the Law of Economy and the Law of Love, you will be qualified to take the next step.

*T*he spiritual life means putting yourself into it. Some effort must be made for spiritual freedom.

We squeeze what we can out of life. We do it through the ability to tune in to Divine Spirit, or the ECK, by singing HU. This is how we come in contact with It.

Not that God lifts our difficulties and our burdens, but God shows us the way to get through them while learning the lessons needed to give us strength. In this way, we become strong enough to walk the road that takes us back home to God.

TOUCHING THE FACE OF GOD

*H*ow do you find God? What makes you yearn for God? It's an indefinable something; and I can only say that often it helps if you have pain, suffering, and loneliness. When life drives you against the wall and you have nowhere else to go, you finally give up trust and confidence in yourself and in your material possessions. And when you can give up attachment and reliance upon anything in the outer world, only then do you have a chance to see the door open for the inner truth of God.

Only then can you find the way to spiritual freedom.

134

*W*e have times when everything is going our way, but there are also times when we're at the bottom. When our fortunes hit bottom, we surrender to Spirit. Then we can go back up more naturally, and we'll maintain this rhythm of life. We are the balanced individual working in the Soul consciousness.

*I*n the spiritual life, we always have to take one more step. These incredible odds come against us, but if we have this ideal set before us—which is Self-Realization or God-Realization—and we keep our attention on it and live our life with common sense, doing the best we can without fear of failure, we will make our way to that ideal.

*I*t's like rising in a hot-air balloon: The higher you go, the more you can see. And the more you can see, the better you are able to arrange your life. Notice I said *you* are better able to arrange your life; it's not me arranging your life. Because really, if you don't care about your life, who else would?

*T*he search for God requires a deep yearning. Soul hears the Voice of God and wants to return to Its home in heaven. In the meantime, it's up to Soul, in one way or another, to find a path that gives the help It needs to take this step.

We are interested in Soul, each one of us. But as we get this understanding, as we become greater in our own unfoldment and move toward the God Consciousness, we also develop many other traits, and compassion is one of them.

I'm not offering you a life of spiritual healings that last forever, because they won't. I'm not offering you a life where prosperity will last forever. It may not. All I am offering you is a glimpse of the face of God, and personal experience in the Light and Sound of this Divine Being.

$\mathcal{H}$eaven is the place where divine love is kept and where divine love flows. It's the heart of God.

*Y*ou're looking for God-Realization, and with this come the attributes of God: wisdom, power, and freedom. But you don't look for the attributes, because when you have the state of God Consciousness, these attributes come with it, as part of the package.

*O*f those who want to walk the spiritual path, I would ask this question: What motivation do you have that is strong enough for you to look for God in every waking moment of your day?

*W*hen an individual looks for God-Realization, it has to be more than a passing fancy. It must be something that is within your heart in a gentle way. You know that no matter what happens on the path, it is always to lead you closer to the source of Soul's creation in the heart of God.

Soul wants to return home, to touch the face of God.

144

About the Author

Author Harold Klemp is known as a pioneer of today's focus on "everyday spirituality." He was raised on a Wisconsin farm and attended divinity school. Then he served in the U.S. Air Force.

In 1981, after years of training, he became the spiritual leader of Eckankar, Religion of the Light and Sound of God. His mission is to help people find their way back to God in this life.

Harold Klemp speaks each year to thousands of seekers at Eckankar seminars. Author of more than sixty books, he continues to write, including many articles and spiritual-study discourses. Harold Klemp's inspiring and practical approach to spirituality helps thousands of people worldwide find greater freedom, wisdom, and love in their lives.

ALSO BY
HAROLD KLEMP

Available at bookstores, online booksellers,
or directly from:
Eckankar
PO Box 2000, Chanhassen, MN 55317-2000 USA.
Tel (952) 380-2222 Fax (952) 380-2196
www.eckankar.org

Immortality of Soul Series
The Language of Soul
Love—The Keystone of Life
Truth Has No Secrets

A selected list:
The Spiritual Exercises of ECK
The Spiritual Laws of Life